THERAPIST AND I

Vonyee Soulfire
Therapist and I

Published by Spines
ISBN: 979-8-89569-526-5

THERAPIST AND I

VONYEE SOULFIRE

To My inner child thank you for pushing me inward. I love you.

Signed:

Adult you

"Everywhere you go There you are!" - Jon Kabat
- You Guided me to healing me. Soulfire

ABOUT JOURNAL

My Therapist and I* is an interactive journal designed to guide you on a transformative journey of self-discovery and healing. This journal delves deep into the profound connection between the mind and body, revealing how our physical experiences are often reflections of our mental and emotional states.

With thought-provoking prompts and exercises, *My Therapist and I* encourages you to explore your inner world, helping you uncover the mental roots of your physical challenges. This journal is not just a place to document your thoughts, but a therapeutic tool to help you bridge the gap between mind and body, ultimately leading to a more holistic understanding of yourself.

Whether you're navigating stress, anxiety, or physical pain, this journal provides a safe space for reflection and growth, empowering you to harness the power of your mind to heal your body. Through consistent journaling, you'll uncover insights that could change the way you understand your well-being, making *My Therapist and I* an essential companion on your path to a healthier, more balanced life.

"*You know what to do, I believe in you.*" Vonyee

HOW TO USE JOURNAL

This Journal is effective when used at the end of every session to record and review comprehension, implementation of tool and strategies to help client continue treatment outside of session. My therapist and I Journal can be uselized withing the last five to ten minutes collective as the therapist view session focus, progress, comprehension of pyscho-education and etc. This double book is combined in one easy to carry and used. It is also digital vision that in a google do share form to together abs easily transferrable to any therapeutic notes tracker. This book is to be use during the last five to ten minutes of session. The book is divided into two part where the client and therapist and celebrated at the same time. They will rap the session together and client will keep the book and return with to back and forth to session. The goal is for the client to be able to have access to relatable resources and tools to deescalate ongoing and new challenges and difficulties that keeps them from living the life and being the person they want. This is your story and I'm honored to provide you a tool to help guide your path your way document by you. It's time you write and tell your story.

I'm horned to serve you.

Vonyee Soulfire, MS, LAC

Illustration by: Danny M

CLIENT

Date Of Entry: ______

Session Number: ______

Therapist Name ______

Topic Disscused: ______

Key Insight: ______

Emotion felt during session: ______

Homework or action items: ______

Question for Next session:

______

Reflection on progress:

______

Personal Notes:

______

Topic Discussed:

______

Work/home stress: ______

Family dynamics: ______

Relationship dynamics: ______

Social support: ______

Core Beliefs: ______

Coping Skills management techniques

______

CLIENT

Date Of Entry: ______________________

Session Number: ______________________

Therapist Name ______________________

Topic Disscused: ______________________

Key Insight: ______________________

Emotion felt during session: ______________________

Homework or action items: ______________________

Question for Next session:

____

Reflection on progress:

____

Personal Notes:

____

Topic Discussed:

____

Work/home stress: ______________________

Family dynamics: ______________________

Relationship dynamics: ______________________

Social support: ______________________

Core Beliefs: ______________________

Coping Skills management techniques

____

CLIENT

Date Of Entry: ______

Session Number: ______

Therapist Name ______

Topic Disscused: ______

Key Insight: ______

Emotion felt during session: ______

Homework or action items: ______

Question for Next session:

______

Reflection on progress:

______

Personal Notes:

______

Topic Discussed:

______

Work/home stress: ______

Family dynamics: ______

Relationship dynamics: ______

Social support: ______

Core Beliefs: ______

Coping Skills management techniques

______

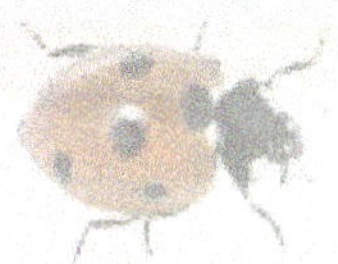

CLIENT

Date Of Entry: ______

Session Number: ______

Therapist Name ______

Topic Disscused: ______

Key Insight: ______

Emotion felt during session: ______

Homework or action items: ______

Question for Next session:

______

Reflection on progress:

______

Personal Notes:

______

Topic Discussed:

______

Work/home stress: ______

Family dynamics: ______

Relationship dynamics: ______

Social support: ______

Core Beliefs: ______

Coping Skills management techniques

______

CLIENT

Date Of Entry: ____________________

Session Number: ____________________

Therapist Name ____________________

Topic Disscused: ____________________

Key Insight: ____________________

Emotion felt during session: ____________________

Homework or action items: ____________________

Question for Next session:

____

Reflection on progress:

____

Personal Notes:

____

Topic Discussed:

____

Work/home stress: ____________________

Family dynamics: ____________________

Relationship dynamics: ____________________

Social support: ____________________

Core Beliefs: ____________________

Coping Skills management techniques

____

CLIENT

Date Of Entry: ______________________________

Session Number: ______________________________

Therapist Name ______________________________

Topic Disscused: ______________________________

Key Insight: ______________________________

Emotion felt during session: ______________________________

Homework or action items: ______________________________

Question for Next session:

____

Reflection on progress:

____

Personal Notes:

____

Topic Discussed:

____

Work/home stress: ______________________________

Family dynamics: ______________________________

Relationship dynamics: ______________________________

Social support: ______________________________

Core Beliefs: ______________________________

Coping Skills management techniques

____

CLIENT

Date Of Entry: ____________________

Session Number: ____________________

Therapist Name ____________________

Topic Disscused: ____________________

Key Insight: ____________________

Emotion felt during session: ____________________

Homework or action items: ____________________

Question for Next session:

____

Reflection on progress:

____

Personal Notes:

____

Topic Discussed:

____

Work/home stress: ____________________

Family dynamics: ____________________

Relationship dynamics: ____________________

Social support: ____________________

Core Beliefs: ____________________

Coping Skills management techniques

____

CLIENT

Date Of Entry: ______

Session Number: ______

Therapist Name ______

Topic Disscused: ______

Key Insight: ______

Emotion felt during session: ______

Homework or action items: ______

Question for Next session:

______

Reflection on progress:

______

Personal Notes:

______

Topic Discussed:

______

Work/home stress: ______

Family dynamics: ______

Relationship dynamics: ______

Social support: ______

Core Beliefs: ______

Coping Skills management techniques

______

CLIENT

Date Of Entry: ______

Session Number: ______

Therapist Name ______

Topic Disscused: ______

Key Insight: ______

Emotion felt during session: ______

Homework or action items: ______

Question for Next session:

______

Reflection on progress:

______

Personal Notes:

______

Topic Discussed:

______

Work/home stress: ______

Family dynamics: ______

Relationship dynamics: ______

Social support: ______

Core Beliefs: ______

Coping Skills management techniques

______

CLIENT

Date Of Entry: ____________________

Session Number: ____________________

Therapist Name ____________________

Topic Disscused: ____________________

Key Insight: ____________________

Emotion felt during session: ____________________

Homework or action items: ____________________

Question for Next session:

____

Reflection on progress:

____

Personal Notes:

____

Topic Discussed:

____

Work/home stress: ____________________

Family dynamics: ____________________

Relationship dynamics: ____________________

Social support: ____________________

Core Beliefs: ____________________

Coping Skills management techniques

____

CLIENT

Date Of Entry: ______________________

Session Number: ______________________

Therapist Name ______________________

Topic Disscused: ______________________

Key Insight: ______________________

Emotion felt during session: ______________________

Homework or action items: ______________________

Question for Next session:

____

Reflection on progress:

____

Personal Notes:

____

Topic Discussed:

____

Work/home stress: ______________________

Family dynamics: ______________________

Relationship dynamics: ______________________

Social support: ______________________

Core Beliefs: ______________________

Coping Skills management techniques

____

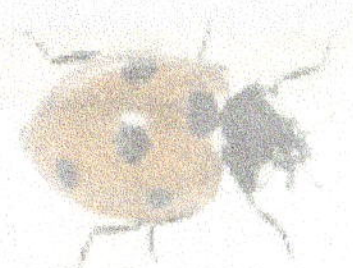

CLIENT

Date Of Entry: ______

Session Number: ______

Therapist Name ______

Topic Disscused: ______

Key Insight: ______

Emotion felt during session: ______

Homework or action items: ______

Question for Next session:

______

Reflection on progress:

______

Personal Notes:

______

Topic Discussed:

______

Work/home stress: ______

Family dynamics: ______

Relationship dynamics: ______

Social support: ______

Core Beliefs: ______

Coping Skills management techniques

______

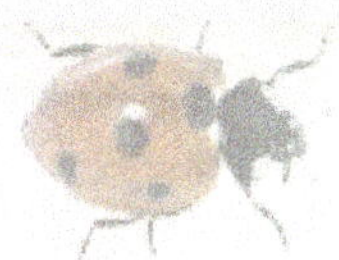

CLIENT

Date Of Entry: ______________________

Session Number: ______________________

Therapist Name ______________________

Topic Disscused: ______________________

Key Insight: ______________________

Emotion felt during session: ______________________

Homework or action items: ______________________

Question for Next session:

____

Reflection on progress:

____

Personal Notes:

____

Topic Discussed:

____

Work/home stress: ______________________

Family dynamics: ______________________

Relationship dynamics: ______________________

Social support: ______________________

Core Beliefs: ______________________

Coping Skills management techniques

____

CLIENT

Date Of Entry: ______

Session Number: ______

Therapist Name ______

Topic Disscused: ______

Key Insight: ______

Emotion felt during session: ______

Homework or action items: ______

Question for Next session:

______

Reflection on progress:

______

Personal Notes:

______

Topic Discussed:

______

Work/home stress: ______

Family dynamics: ______

Relationship dynamics: ______

Social support: ______

Core Beliefs: ______

Coping Skills management techniques

______

CLIENT

Date Of Entry: ______________________

Session Number: ______________________

Therapist Name ______________________

Topic Disscused: ______________________

Key Insight: ______________________

Emotion felt during session: ______________________

Homework or action items: ______________________

Question for Next session:

____

Reflection on progress:

____

Personal Notes:

____

Topic Discussed:

____

Work/home stress: ______________________

Family dynamics: ______________________

Relationship dynamics: ______________________

Social support: ______________________

Core Beliefs: ______________________

Coping Skills management techniques

____

THERAPIST

Date Of Entry: ____________________

Client Name ID: ____________________

Session Number: ____________________

Topic Disscused: ____________________

Therapeutic intervention used

____

Client response to intervention:

____

Progress observed:

____

Challenged faced: ____________________

Next step/ treatment plan

____

Notte on client emotional state

Self refection on the session:

____

THERAPIST

Date Of Entry: ______

Client Name ID: ______

Session Number: ______

Topic Disscused: ______

Therapeutic intervention used

______

Client response to intervention:

______

Progress observed:

______

Challenged faced: ______

Next step/ treatment plan

______

Notte on client emotional state

Self refection on the session:

______

THERAPIST

Date Of Entry: ______

Client Name ID: ______

Session Number: ______

Topic Disscused: ______

Therapeutic intervention used

______

Client response to intervention:

______

Progress observed:

______

Challenged faced: ______

Next step/ treatment plan

______

Notte on client emotional state

Self refection on the session:

______

THERAPIST

Date Of Entry:

Client Name ID:

Session Number:

Topic Disscused:

Therapeutic intervention used

Client response to intervention:

Progress observed:

Challenged faced:

Next step/ treatment plan

Notte on client emotional state

Self refection on the session:

THERAPIST

Date Of Entry:

Client Name ID:

Session Number:

Topic Disscused:

Therapeutic intervention used

Client response to intervention:

Progress observed:

Challenged faced:

Next step/ treatment plan

Notte on client emotional state

Self refection on the session:

THERAPIST

Date Of Entry: ____________________

Client Name ID: ____________________

Session Number: ____________________

Topic Disscused: ____________________

Therapeutic intervention used

____

Client response to intervention:

____

Progress observed:

____

Challenged faced: ____________________

Next step/ treatment plan

____

Notte on client emotional state

Self refection on the session:

____

THERAPIST

Date Of Entry: ____________________

Client Name ID: ____________________

Session Number: ____________________

Topic Disscused: ____________________

Therapeutic intervention used

____

Client response to intervention:

____

Progress observed:

____

Challenged faced: ____________________

Next step/ treatment plan

____

Notte on client emotional state

Self refection on the session:

____

THERAPIST

Date Of Entry: ______________________

Client Name ID: ______________________

Session Number: ______________________

Topic Disscused: ______________________

Therapeutic intervention used

____

Client response to intervention:

____

Progress observed:

____

Challenged faced: ______________________

Next step/ treatment plan

____

Notte on client emotional state

Self refection on the session:

____

THERAPIST

Date Of Entry: ____________________

Client Name ID: ____________________

Session Number: ____________________

Topic Disscused: ____________________

Therapeutic intervention used

Client response to intervention:

Progress observed:

Challenged faced: ____________________

Next step/ treatment plan

Notte on client emotional state

Self refection on the session:

THERAPIST

Date Of Entry:

Client Name ID:

Session Number:

Topic Disscused:

Therapeutic intervention used

Client response to intervention:

Progress observed:

Challenged faced:

Next step/ treatment plan

Notte on client emotional state

Self refection on the session:

THERAPIST

Date Of Entry:

Client Name ID:

Session Number:

Topic Disscused:

Therapeutic intervention used

Client response to intervention:

Progress observed:

Challenged faced:

Next step/ treatment plan

Notte on client emotional state

Self refection on the session:

THERAPIST

Date Of Entry: ______________________

Client Name ID: ______________________

Session Number: ______________________

Topic Disscused: ______________________

Therapeutic intervention used

____

Client response to intervention:

____

Progress observed:

____

Challenged faced: ______________________

Next step/ treatment plan

____

Notte on client emotional state

Self refection on the session:

____

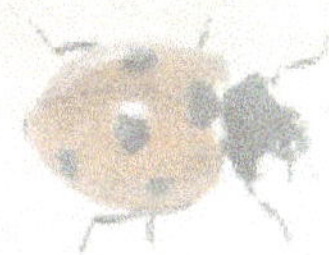

THERAPIST

Date Of Entry: ____________________

Client Name ID: ____________________

Session Number: ____________________

Topic Disscused: ____________________

Therapeutic intervention used

____

Client response to intervention:

____

Progress observed:

____

Challenged faced: ____________________

Next step/ treatment plan

____

Notte on client emotional state

Self refection on the session:

____

THERAPIST

Date Of Entry: ______

Client Name ID: ______

Session Number: ______

Topic Disscused: ______

Therapeutic intervention used

______

Client response to intervention:

______

Progress observed:

______

Challenged faced: ______

Next step/ treatment plan

______

Notte on client emotional state

Self refection on the session:

______

THERAPIST

Date Of Entry: ____

Client Name ID: ____

Session Number: ____

Topic Disscused: ____

Therapeutic intervention used

____

Client response to intervention:

____

Progress observed:

____

Challenged faced: ____

Next step/ treatment plan

____

Notte on client emotional state

Self refection on the session:

____

DAILY REFLECTIONS

Date:

Events:

What Are you grateful for today?

What did you do right today?

What are you looking forward to Tomorrow?

DAILY REFLECTIONS

Date:

Events:

What Are you grateful for today?

What did you do right today?

What are you looking forward to Tomorrow?

DAILY REFLECTIONS

Date:

Events:

What Are you grateful for today?

What did you do right today?

What are you looking forward to Tomorrow?

DAILY REFLECTIONS

Date:

Events:

What Are you grateful for today?

What did you do right today?

What are you looking forward to Tomorrow?

DAILY REFLECTIONS

Date:

Events:

What Are you grateful for today?

What did you do right today?

What are you looking forward to Tomorrow?

DAILY REFLECTIONS

Date:

Events:

What Are you grateful for today?

What did you do right today?

What are you looking forward to Tomorrow?

DAILY REFLECTIONS

Date:

Events:

What Are you grateful for today?

What did you do right today?

What are you looking forward to Tomorrow?

DAILY REFLECTIONS

Date:

Events:

What Are you grateful for today?

What did you do right today?

What are you looking forward to Tomorrow?

DAILY REFLECTIONS

Date:

Events:

What Are you grateful for today?

What did you do right today?

What are you looking forward to Tomorrow?

DAILY REFLECTIONS

Date:

Events:

What Are you grateful for today?

What did you do right today?

What are you looking forward to Tomorrow?

DAILY REFLECTIONS

Date:

Events:

What Are you grateful for today?

What did you do right today?

What are you looking forward to Tomorrow?

DAILY REFLECTIONS

Date:

Events:

What Are you grateful for today?

What did you do right today?

What are you looking forward to Tomorrow?

DAILY REFLECTIONS

Date:

Events:

What Are you grateful for today?

What did you do right today?

What are you looking forward to Tomorrow?

DAILY REFLECTIONS

Date:

Events:

What Are you grateful for today?

What did you do right today?

What are you looking forward to Tomorrow?

DAILY REFLECTIONS

Date:

Events:

What Are you grateful for today?

What did you do right today?

What are you looking forward to Tomorrow?

www.ingramcontent.com/pod-product-compliance
Lightning Source LLC
LaVergne TN
LVHW050424160826
845677LV00002BA/515

* 9 7 9 8 8 9 5 6 9 5 2 6 5 *